?

The
WORST-CASE SCENARIO
Survival Handbook:
Middle School

The
WORST-CASE SCENARIO
Survival Handbook:
Middle School

By David Borgenicht, Ben H. Winters, and Robin Epstein

Illustrated by Chuck Gonzales

A⁺
Smart Apple Media

A WORD OF WARNING: It's always important to keep safety in mind. If you're careless, even the tamest activities can result in injury. As such, all readers are urged to act with caution, ask for adult advice, obey all laws, and respect the rights of others when handling any Worst-Case Scenario.

Published by Smart Apple Media, an imprint of Black Rabbit Books
P.O. Box 3263, Mankato, Minnesota 56002
www.blackrabbitbooks.com

This library-bound edition is reprinted by arrangement with Chronicle Books, LLC, 680 Second Street, San Francisco, California 94107

First Published in the United States in 2009 by Chronicle Books LLC.

A QUIRK PACKAGING BOOK.

Worst-Case Scenario® and The Worst-Case Scenario Survival Handbook™ are trademarks of Quirk Productions, Inc.

Book design by Lynne Yeamans.
Typeset in Adobe Garamond, Blockhead, and Imperfect.
Illustrations by Chuck Gonzales.

Library of Congress Cataloging-in-Publication Data
The worst-case scenario survival handbook : middle school / David Borgenicht, Ben H. Winters, and Robin Epstein.
     pages cm
  ISBN 978-1-59920-977-7
1. Middle school students--Life skills guides. 2. Preteens--Life skills guides. 3. Teenagers--Life skills guides. 4. Middle schools--Humor. I. Winters, Ben H. II. Epstein, Robin, 1972-
  LB1135.B66 2015
  373.18--dc23
                              2013037223

Printed in the United States at Corporate Graphics,
North Mankato, Minnesota, 2-2014, PO 1644
10 9 8 7 6 5 4 3 2 1

CONTENTS

Introduction

Stuck in the middle...

The middle of nowhere...

Middle age...

Sometimes being "in the middle" gets a bad rap. But if you're in the middle—or about to *start* the middle—of your school career, there's actually a lot to look forward to...*if* you're prepared.

This handbook is your very own insider's guide to the unique world that is middle school. It's kind of like getting a sneak peek at the teacher's edition of your math book. It doesn't have all the answers to your next test, but it *does* have all the tips and secrets you need to make the most of that oh-so-special time in the middle.

So, what exactly *is* so special about middle school? One word: CHANGE.

Middle school is one of those times in life when a whole lotta change happens in a pretty short time. In those middle years, people get taller, they get new interests, their social lives change, and their minds start thinking in more and more sophisticated ways. It's one big chapter of change.

And it's not just about what happens *during* middle school—the chapter *begins* with a big whammy of a change, too. When you start middle school, you're fresh out of elementary school. Back there, you were old and wise. You knew the ropes. You knew the rules. There were plenty of short people around to make you feel tall. But then, along comes middle school and suddenly, BANG! You're in opposite land. You're a newbie. A young'un! Lots of things are different—the way your classes are set up, what's expected of you, the way your friends act, everything!

This book is here to help you navigate that sea of change. It'll help prepare you for the choppy waters—and sharks!—so you'll have plenty of time for smooth middle-school sailing. Here's how this handbook can help:

- *Nervous about the school dance? We have the moves to get you through.*

- *Prepping for a big test? You'll find plenty of tried and true studying hints in here.*

- *Have a sinking grade? We toss you a lifeline.*

- *Dealing with a bully or mean girl? We give you the upper hand.*

- *Being crushed by a crush? We show you how to read the signs.*

- *Growing apart from your best friend? We help you deal—* and *make new friends.*

Whether you're a middle-school rookie or a seasoned pro, the tips, tricks, and secrets you'll find inside this handbook will help you have an amazing year (or two, or three). Now, it's time to dig in and get to the juicy *middle* of things!

—David Borgenicht, Ben H. Winters, and Robin Epstein

CHAPTER 1

The School Day

How to Survive Day One

If middle school were a game, the first day would be like the championship. Here's how to be in it to win it.

1 Conduct an investigation.

Does your school have a website? Check it out! Can you tour the school in advance? Do it! Know kids who already attend? Ask them for insider information! If you know what to expect, you'll keep the pre-game jitters at bay.

2 Look great, feel great.

Take your first-day clothes for a test drive a few weeks beforehand to make sure they look and feel right. You can even host your own fashion show by asking your best bud for an opinion. Knowing you look your best will help you have the confidence you need.

3 Buddy up.

Find out who's in your homeroom, who you can walk to gym with, and whose fries you can "borrow" in the cafeteria. Plan ahead to maximize "friend" time.

4 Map quest.

If you don't have a map of your school, make one. Add crucial information like a route from gym to math that takes you past a water fountain.

5 Imagine success.

See yourself being happy, making friends, and feeling great. Don't let yourself imagine an uncomfortable you. The better you visualize your day, the better you can make it.

The Locker Lowdown

Think of your locker as your home base, your fortress, your space to decorate or mess up as you see fit!

- Memorize your combo with a little poem like, "47, 13, 4, that's the combo I adore."

- Do a once-a-month super-clean. Toss what you don't need and organize the rest.

- Make sure dirty clothes don't hang around—they have a way of "ripening" in small, dark spaces.

- Keep a little mirror for between-class hair fixes and to check for paint smudges on your cheeks after art class.

- Avoid storing food "for later," which might turn into "for the roaches that have moved in and are now quite comfortable."

How to Keep Track of All Your Business

Read this list, then close your eyes and repeat it: For first period, answer questions 12 through 27. For second period, read chapters 5 through 7. For third period, do worksheet 6. For fifth period, do problems 6 through 13, skipping 8 and 11.

If it was tough to remember that list *now*, it'll be even tougher at the end of a school day, when your brain feels like a wet noodle. Enter the homework planner, a.k.a. your brain saver!

1 ## Save the plan-it!

Assignments and quizzes and tests, oh my! Avoid getting lost in the woods by making (or buying) a planner where you can jot down crucial class info. Choose a notebook that's not too bulky— you'll be carrying this baby *everywhere*. Set up each page in your planner like the example on the next page.

2 Love your planner.

Record *everything* in there—not just homework and tests, but also upcoming field trips, long-term projects, and friends' birthdays. (Who doesn't like to be remembered on their birthday?!)

3 Get all the deets, all the time.

Make sure to record all the details as your teacher announces an assignment. If you're going to do the work, you want to make sure you're doing the right stuff.

SUBJECT	MONDAY 3/22	TUESDAY 3/23	WEDNESDAY 3/24
MATH		P. 39 (#22-46, EVENS)	
ENGLISH			STUDY CH. 5-6 VOCAB
SCIENCE	TEST ON UNIT 4		
SOCIAL STUDIES			DEFINE CHAPTER 3 KEY TERMS
ART		BRING POSTERBOARD	
AFTER SCHOOL	SOCCER PRACTICE 4:00		GABE'S BIRTHDAY!

Write down all the details.

Record friends' birthdays.

4 Check, please!

As you pack your bag for the trip home, give your planner a final check so you can pack any books you'll need to get your homework done. Leave the others in your locker so they don't weigh you down.

5 Do one final prep.

The next morning, check that planner again. If you've got football practice, pack your helmet. If there's a field trip, bring a snack. If it's Saturday, don't go to school!

THURSDAY 3/25	FRIDAY 3/26	WEEKEND 3/27–28
	FIELD TRIP (ALL DAY) TO SCIENCE MUSEUM!	
VOCAB QUIZ		GET STARTED ON BOOK REPORT
		STUDY GROUP FOR TEST
Check your planner before you leave home to be sure you have everything.		
SOCCER PRACTICE 4:00		WASH GYM CLOTHES!

How to Fix a Problem with a Teacher

Maybe it feels like you're the *only* one who gets called out for being late. Maybe the *one time* you toss your friend a note, your teacher catches it. Or maybe you feel like he just has it in for you. If you sense that you and your teacher aren't clicking, try pushing these buttons instead.

Do   Don't

① Find a time to talk...privately.

Politely ask your teacher if there's a time when you two can speak privately, so you won't feel rushed. Good times to talk: during lunch, after school. Bad times: as your teacher passes your desk while handing out home-work, right before the bell rings.

② Nod a lot.

Arrive to your meeting on time and start by saying something like, "I want to talk about what I can do to help us get along better." You made the brave move of taking that first step. Now you gotta see it through—look your teacher in the eyes while he's talking, and don't squirm, slouch, or look at the clock!

> **BE AWARE** • Slow nodding says, "I'm listening," and signals that you're taking your teacher seriously. Too-fast nodding says, "Okay, I get it, enough already!"

③ Resist the urge to debate.

Every time you say, "I didn't do that," or, "He's lying!" you keep the conversation in the past—and the past

is the place where you kept getting in trouble. Try forward-looking statements like, "What can I do to succeed?," or, "I'd love for us to have a fresh start. How can I make that happen?"

④ Make conversational extra credit.

Before you leave, make sure to thank your teacher for taking the time to talk to you. Expressing your gratitude lets you walk out with your best foot forward!

How to Rescue a Sinking Grade

Your geography grade is sinking like it's caught in quicksand in Morecambe Bay. (And if you weren't tanking in geography, you'd know where that is.) You need someone to throw you a lifeline, quick…and here it is.

1 Hold a strategy session.

The learning process is like a game of tug-of-war. The more folks you have on your side, the better your chance to win. Feel like you're getting pulled down? Recruit help! Let your teacher know you'd like to do

better, and ask her to help you come up with a plan for success. Maybe she can recommend a tutor or fellow student who can help you out.

② Twenty questions.

If a concept isn't sinking in, ask a question. Still don't get it? Ask another question. Then ask another person! Don't give up till you find someone who can explain the confusing stuff in a way that makes sense to you.

③ Build your own A-Team.

Your friend's a science whiz. You're a budding Shake-speare. So, do like Billy S. himself, and "swappeth skills." Have Mr. Wizard help you with your lab project, and you help him with his "book learnin'."

④ Ask for an extra-credit card.

You never know until you ask, so don't wait another minute: Ask your teacher if you can do something to score extra points. Maybe you can do another math worksheet? Write a short story using vocab words? Make a science poster explaining photosynthesis? It never hurts to make a suggestion!

How to Play It Cool When You Don't Know the Answer

You are *the* French master! You can conjugate *être* upside down and backward! So naturally, the one time you're called on in French class is the one time you left your *livre* in your locker the night before. Anyone know the word for "help" *en français*?

1. Take a moment.

Getting called on by surprise can make you panic. Take control! You don't have to answer right away, even though all eyes are on you. Take a deep breath, think back to your homework or your textbook, and give it your best shot. If you really can't come up with anything, then…

2. Be honest.

Look right back at the teacher and say, "Sorry, I don't know that one." At worst, you'll get reprimanded for not paying attention. At best, you'll get points for being honest. Earn cred in a foreign-language class by saying "I don't know" in the language that's stumped you.

3. Tip it over to a smart pal.

If it's a fraction you're stuck on, and your pal is Miss Fractions, try a little alley-oop: "I don't know, but I betcha Emily does." Just be careful: If Emily's knowledge is more fractional than you think, she's going to be plenty peeved that you shifted the spotlight onto *her*.

4 Raise your hand when you *do* know the answer.

Just like people take vitamin C to help ward off a cold, you can prevent the dreaded "getting called on when you're clueless." Teachers just want to hear from you, so participate early and often when you *do* know the answer. That should reduce your chances of getting called on when you *don't*.

How to Challenge a Cheater

They say that cheaters never win and winners never cheat, but how does that help *you* if someone's trying to harness your brainpower?

SCENARIO 1

You sacrificed watching your favorite TV show to finish your math homework. But when you get on the bus, a greedy homework hog asks to copy your work.

① Just say no.

Don't even listen to the cheater's pleas for help. Say "no can do" to that h-work hog, pop in your ear buds, and take a seat. Simple as that.

② Try a quick comeback.

If the cheater won't buzz off, use one of these replies:

- *"I finished the assignment in school yesterday and already turned it in."*
- *"That's so funny—I was just about to ask to cheat off you!"*
- *"Actually, my dog barfed on it. You sure you want to touch it? I guess it doesn't smell too bad…"*

SCENARIO 2

You studied like crazy for the history test and now know more about Columbus than C. C.'s mother did. But the test pest to your left is trying to steal the words right off your answer sheet.

① Go on the move.

Ask for a different seat on the opposite side of the room. No need to tattle: Say your chair is squeaking or the sun's in your eyes.

❷ Play a little defense.

Block your paper with your forearm, or let your scratch paper just *happen* to cover up your answers.

> **BE AWARE** • Sometimes blocking your paper isn't enough. If you still see those prying eyes, don't hesitate to tell the teacher after class.

WORST NIGHTMARE

I'VE BEEN ACCUSED OF CHEATING...AND I DIDN'T DO IT!

Yes, your eyes were wandering—they *always* do that!—but you truly weren't cheating, honest! What if you're falsely charged?

- **Remain calm.** Crying or getting angry only makes you look guilty.

- **Offer to retake the test.** If you can ace it again on the spot, you'll prove your point.

- **Talk yourself up.** You turn in homework on time. You read independently. Basically, you're too smart to cheat!

How to Survive Getting in Trouble

Maybe you were passing notes in class, running in the hallway, or listening to your headphones under your hood. It seemed worth it at the time, but now that you've been busted, you're not so sure. You're queasy, your hands are sweating, and the room is spinning before your eyes. Do you need the school nurse? Nope—you need to check out these miracle cures.

① **Tell the truth.**

Here's a simple formula you won't learn in math: Getting in trouble + Lying about it = Much worse trouble. If you were texting in class, admit it and move on.

② **Don't fight fire with fire.**

You weren't the only one peeking at the teachers' edition, but you can keep that information to yourself. Tattling on the others won't lessen your punishment.

③ **Keep your lips zipped.**

Adults *love* it when you talk back, don't they? (*Yeah*, about as much as getting a bee sting on the bohunkus.) Don't be that bee! When you're getting a "talking to," maintain respectful silence so you won't cause more trouble than you already have.

④ **Think about next week.**

Seven days from now, this will just be a bad memory. Your body may be sitting on that hard bench outside the principal's office *today*, but in your mind you can already be playing video games or hanging out at the mall, with your punishment (way) behind you.

Five Ways to Pass the Time in Detention

With every minute stretching out in front of you like hot pizza cheese, detention can feel like it lasts a lifetime—unless you stop staring at the clock and try one of these sanity savers.

- **If you're a righty, try writing the alphabet with your left hand.** If you're a lefty, write righty.

- **Test your ESP.** Can you move an object with your mind? Can you influence someone else's thoughts through yours? You will try it now…

- **Think about what you did to get detention.** Then try to figure out how you could have done it *without* getting caught.

- **Make detention work for you.** If you're allowed to do your homework, get busy so you don't have to waste precious free time slaving over it later.

How to Survive the Locker-Room Change

Pants (and shirt!) off—in front of your classmates? *Yikes!* If just the thought of doing the costume change for gym class gives you stage fright, try a few of these tricks to ease your performance anxiety.

OPTION 1: Turn away and make it quick.

1 Face your locker instead of the crowd.

Stand as close to your gym locker as possible without actually climbing in.

2 Get all your gym clothes ready *before* the old ones come off.

Make sure you've got everything you need (from shorts to shirt to socks), so you're not rooting around in your bag without pants on. As soon as everything is laid out in a clothing assembly line: presto-change-o! The process will fly by.

3. Dress in pieces.

Instead of getting fully undressed, approach it one article of clothing at a time. Take off your pants—then pull on your gym shorts. Next, replace your regular shirt with your gym shirt. Continue until you're all suited up.

4. Be a speed demon.

Glance at your watch before you start undressing, and see if you can set a personal record for a clothing change. If you're moving at the speed of light, no one can see a thing.

OPTION 2: Squeeze in your social hour.

Conversation is a natural distraction, so yak it up with your friends as you change. Talk about the crazy tricks your pets can do, the awesome gadget you want for your birthday, the class that's driving you bonkers... whatever. Soon enough, you'll be all changed without having to spend a minute thinking about it.

OPTION 3: Plain white Ts to the rescue.

You might feel less exposed if you wear a light undershirt beneath your school clothes. That way, when you're changing into your gym uniform, you can stay wrapped in a protective layer.

OPTION 4: Use the "stalling" technique.

If all else fails, head for a bathroom stall and do your thing in your own private dressing room. If anybody asks what you were doing in there, look at them like they're crazy: "Uh, it's a bathroom—what do you *think* I was doing?"

CHAPTER 2

After School

How to Scale a Mountain of Homework

The worst part of running up a hill is when you're at the bottom, just *thinking* about running up the hill. The same is true for homework, so stop the head games and *just do it*! Here's how to gear up and ascend to success.

1 Feed your brain.

Before you get started, give yourself a "head" start on homework by snacking on "smart food" (nuts, fruit, veggies, popcorn). Healthy fuel will make your brain run better.

2 "X" marks the homework spot.

Seek out a super-comfortable, bright, quiet place to make your personal workstation. Decorate it to inspire you and remind you of your triumphs. If the homework spot is a place you like going to, the whole experience will improve. (You may even look forward to it!)

③ Distractions, keep out!

Turn off the TV. Put your phone in the cupboard behind the food you hate most. The faster you focus, the sooner you'll get the job done.

④ Beat the clock.

Deadlines make adrenaline flow! If you know you need to finish a task by a certain time, your body will rise to the challenge. Set a realistic amount of time to finish, like, "I'll finish my homework by 4 PM," then set an alarm. Victory (a.k.a. completed homework) will soon be yours!

5 Break fast.

Every twenty to thirty minutes, take a break. Stand up, shake out your limbs, do whatever makes you feel human again. A short burst of movement gives your body a breather, so you can hit the remaining work like a hammer.

Finished Homework Rewards

Know what's better than finishing your homework? *Getting a reward for doing it!* Promise to do something you love when you're done and you'll have extra incentive to finish fast.

1. Ride your bike around the neighborhood knowing you're free at last!

2. Find the funniest clips online and laugh for as long as you want.

3. Call your friend—and you *don't* have to talk about homework!

4. Try getting to the next level on your fave video game.

5. If it's sugar you crave, give yourself a little. You've earned it!

How to Prep for a Test in Your Toughest Class

No one, but *no one* likes tests. Know why? 'Cause they "test" you! It can feel like someone's poking you in the head, squeezing your brain like it's a melon at the market. Here are a few test-taking tips that'll stop you from going bananas.

1 Pool brainpower.

Harness your friends' superpower smarts by studying together. Allison is the fractions master, but Raviv is an expert at prime numbers. You need 'em both around to get an A on the killer math test.

2 Host a game show.

Change the mood from "ugh, test coming" to "we're hanging out and having fun!" This will let your poor, stressed-out brain relax and absorb the material. Make a mic out of a hairbrush or spoon and take turns being the game-show host. See who can answer the fastest. If you're stumped, just hearing the answer from your friends will help to stick it in your brain.

3 Transform into your teacher (only temporarily, don't worry).

Ever wonder why your history teacher knows so much about history? It's because teaching something is the best way to learn it. Once you get a section of the material cracked, teach it to one of your study buds, or unleash your wisdom on a family member.

A CELL HAS RIBOSOMES, THAT LOOK LIKE TINY LITTLE DOMES, THEY'RE MADE OF STUFF CALLED RNA, AND THEY MAKE PROTEIN EVERY DAY!

4 Create your own mnemonic devices.

If you have to memorize a poem and present it to the class, put it to the tune of your favorite song. When it's your day to present, sing each line in your head first, then say it out loud (unless you want to make it a *truly* memorable musical performance!). Even vocab words are easy to remember if you make up sentences like, "The *hirsute* old man looked like he was wearing a hair suit."

Secrets of the Multiple-Choice Masters

The good news is that the answer is right before your eyes. All you need to do is choose it! Here's how.

1. **Read the question twice.** Read the question twice. Now you've probably already thought of the answer before looking at the options.

2. **Off with their heads!** Immediately cross out the answers you *know* are wrong, then pick the best of the rest.

3. **If two choices are opposites,** then one of them is probably completely, totally, and awesomely wrong, making the other…Bingo!

4. **Teachers rarely give "trick questions,"** so don't try to out-think the test-maker, or else your head might get twisted up in knots.

5. **Go with your gut.** It lets you know when you're hungry—trust that it'll help guide you here, too!

QUIZ

1 (A) (B) (C)
2 (A) (B) (C)
3 (A) (B) (C)
4 (A) (B) (C)
5 (A) (B) (C)
6 (A) (B) (C)
7 (A) (B) (C)
8 (A) (B) (C)

How to Survive a Group Assignment

If two heads are better than one, think how much higher the "better factor" goes when you get to work in a group. Applying multiple minds means work gets divided up and done faster, and chances are you'll wind up doing the part you like or know best. Here are some ways to keep the team working like an elite crew of taskmasters.

1 Split skills.

Everyone should have a job and know her part. Pick (or elect) a leader if it makes sense to do so, then draft a list of names, roles, and due dates. The more organized you can be from the start, the faster you'll get to the end.

2 Power to the people...

When discussing your group-project plans, let everyone speak. Some people are going to be quieter than others, but that doesn't mean they don't have interesting ideas. Encourage Silent Bob to speak up by going around the circle and getting *everyone's* opinion.

3 There's no such thing as a bad idea.

Especially during the brainstorming phase, let every idea flow. Avoid dismissing or criticizing suggestions, because that will make people clam up. An idea that might seem strange at the start may well be a stroke of genius—or could inspire one—if you allow yourself to ponder it.

4 ## Use the wisdom of crowds.

If your group disagrees on how to attack a problem or the best way to present an answer, be democratic and encourage a vote. Debate the issues, let each side have its say, then let the group decide. Your group motto? "Everyone has a voice."

5 ## Take on slackers...positively.

Sometimes a group member will avoid doing his fair share. Instead of getting mad at the person (which will only make him want to work less... *if that's even possible!*), engage him in a *positive* way. Talk to him about the task he was assigned, then ask if he needs any help or if he would prefer to work on another part of the project. Focus on how the group needs his contribution, not on what he's doing wrong.

BE AWARE • Occasionally, no matter how much you encourage a certain teammate, that person might disappoint you, forcing you to step in and pick up some of the slack. If that happens, continue to involve Kid Slacker so he not only contributes *something*, but he also knows he owes you one!

The Leader of the Pack

Even the shyest person can become a great group leader. Here's how.

- **Come into the first meeting with a basic schedule.** Make a plan, even if that might change down the line. People are likely to follow someone who seems prepared.

- **Flattery will get you everywhere.** Try lines like, "You're such a good artist—it would be so cool if our very own Picasso could do this poster for us!"

- **Be positive.** Instead of, "That cover page is pathetic," try, "Great start. Why don't we all think of ways to improve it?"

- **Don't get carried away.** No matter how good a leader you are, the group is not going to clean out your locker, wash your gym uniform, or feed your fish.

How to Try Out Without Freaking Out

After-school activities are great for making friends, blowing off steam, and showing off skills (and putting off homework!). But making the team or auditioning for the play can be intimidating. Here's how to send those nerves packing and enjoy the ride.

MAKING THE TEAM

- Just as you train your brain for a test, you can give your body a boost before tryouts. Start exercising and practicing now to prepare.
- When the big day arrives, prove that you'll make a great teammate by cheering for others, too.

NABBING A PART IN THE SCHOOL PLAY

- Before you arrive, look up the show online so you know as much as possible about it. If it's a musical, find out if you'll have to sing at the audition. Then be a rock star: Pick a song, memorize it, and practice your heart out!
- As you audition, pretend you've already made it. Think of the people in the room as your enthusiastic opening-night audience.

GETTING ON THE CHEERLEADING SQUAD

- Cheerleading is all about attitude. A big smile can be as valuable as a back handspring.
- Ask someone who's on the squad to teach you a cheer or two so you can walk into the tryout one high kick ahead of the curve.

RUNNING FOR STUDENT OFFICE

- Campaigning is key, so arrive to school early during the week before the election and say "hey" to everyone coming into the building. Think of a memorable slogan, and use that theme in all your campaign materials. For instance, if you say, "Jimmy has the magic!" you could hand out playing cards with your name and campaign plans on them.
- During your speech, you could do a magic trick. Keep hitting that message: You have the power to get things done!

Worst Nightmare

Your buds made the team and now they're busy doing the one thing you wish you could do. There *are* ways to make this major bummer better.

ALL MY FRIENDS MADE THE TEAM, BUT I DIDN'T!

• Take note.

What moves did your friends make that got them on the team? Work on those for next year's tryouts!

• Cheer 'em on.

Instead of feeling left out, "join the team" in other ways. Sit in the front row of the bleachers when your pals are playing, and cheer louder than anyone else. Bonus: Being a good observer of the team's strategies will reveal helpful tricks *you* can put to use.

• Try something else.

Maybe you're not destined to be a star soccer player—what about being your school's first-ever fencing champion? How 'bout starting a comedy troupe? Ask an administrator how you can start your own group, team, or club—and make your own fun!

How to Survive a Massive Mess-Up

You did it! You did it! You kicked the ball right into the net! Except, uh, that's the other team's net, and you just scored a goal for the *visitors.* Or maybe you tossed a total air ball on your foul shot, or shouted at full volume when all the other cheerleaders were totally silent. Your extracurricular just got extra embarrassing, but it's nothing you can't handle.

1. Minimize the damage.

If you spaced on your big line in the play, make up something "in character" to say. If your pom-pom flew into the bleachers, keep cheering with the other one.

2. Fake it.

No matter how much you feel like collapsing in tears, keep playing (or cheering, or acting) with a smile. Freaking out will tell the world that this *is* a big deal. If you stay calm, they may never know.

3. Tease yourself first.

You know the jokes are coming, so get there first with one of these self-directed zingers.

- *"Just trying to keep things interesting."*
- *"So did everyone see my lesson on what* not *to do?"*
- *"Well, let's not run that play again."*

4. Learn from your mistakes.

Do you need to rehearse more? Practice a particular move? If your next performance is terrific, no one will remember the time you kicked the goalie instead of the ball.

Benched!

You're on the team, but Coach never plays you. Or you're in the play, but instead of Leading Lady, you're Shrub #4. Here's how to make the best of it.

- **Be helpful**: Hand out towels, pour water, or, while you're waiting to rehearse Shrub #4's scene, grab a brush and paint scenery. That way, you're involved and useful.

- **Branch out**: After practice, work on your handmade-jewelry line or teach yourself to juggle. Once you find other stuff you're good at, it won't matter if you're not so hot on the field.

How to Avoid Extra-Curricular Exhaustion

You joined three teams, four clubs, pep band, and debate. When you're debating whether to nap in social studies or math class, it's time to drop out of *something*. Move the following assignment to the top of today's list: Get Mom and Dad to give you the okay.

1 Pick the right time to discuss the drop.

This is *not* a conversation to have right after practice, when you're worn out, grumpy, and irritated. That only hands Mom and Dad an easy response: "You had a rough day. Try again tomorrow."

2 Make a list of pros and cons.

Write the list out twice, so each parent can have a copy. Note the benefits of staying involved with the activity to show your folks that you're not *only* seeing negatives: You've thought it over and made a mature decision.

SWIMMING

PROS
- cute bathing suits
- future lifeguard training
- will be able to out-swim sharks at the beach
- good for my "character"

Cons
- green hair, red eyes
- freezing cold water
- early morning wake-up
- falling asleep in math class

③ Arrive armed with answers.

Anticipate what your parents might say and prepare good responses in advance.

Parents: *"You need to give field hockey more of a chance."*

You: *"I talked to my coach about that, and she felt that three months was long enough to get a good sense of the sport."*

Parents: *"Learning an instrument is important."*

You: *"Having enough study time is even more important."*

Do *not* say:

"I'm so bad at the oboe, it just sounds like I'm farting!"

"Maybe if you got your lazy behind off the couch and practiced with me, I'd be better."

"But you quit everything you start, Dad!"

CHAPTER 3

The Social Scene

How to Be Truly Popular

Dirty little secret: People who think they belong to the "popular crowd" have it *backward.*

It's not a "crowd" if it's only a few people. Plus, true popularity means having lots of friends—*not* excluding them.

HOW TO BUILD YOUR CIRCLE

1 Be an inquiring mind.

Want to get to know someone new? Start with a question like, "What'd you think of that English assignment?" "Did you read that book?" "Cool (shirt/shoes/pants), where'd you get it/them?" "What's for lunch?"

> **BE AWARE** • If your "way in" goes *way* badly, no biggie. Blow it off with a comment like, "Take your time, it was a tough question," or "I like how you answered that with a nonanswer. Are you hoping for a career in politics?"

2 Show your interest.

As you get to know this new person, show interest in what he's saying by listening well and asking follow-up questions. Delve deeper with "why" questions, like, "Why'd you decide to play trumpet?"

3 Add water.

As the friendship grows, suggest getting together outside of school for a movie, skateboarding session, or sleepover.

4 Smile more, smile often.

Flashing a smile is like starting a private conversation. Grinning not only says, "I'm a nice person, come say hi!" it also lets people know you're *not* judge-y. Just think about how it'll feel to have loads of pals, and that smile'll spread naturally.

5 Are you positive? Say yes!

Remember: It's more fun to hang out with someone who's upbeat and positive than it is to hang out with Hater McWhineypants.

6 Be a uniter.

You have friends scattered in all parts of your life—from school, outside activities, summer camp, etc. So if you want to hang with a larger group, do some community organizing. Invite all your peeps to a party. Bringing different groups of friends together is what a real leader does.

7 Know your true friends.

A group is great, but one quality amigo—a partner in crime who's there when you need to talk serious stuff—is priceless. (Be sure to treat him that way!)

How to Remake Your Rep

Middle school is like the next level up in a video game: You get a clean screen, new powers, and the chance to turn yourself into the person you've always wanted to be. Once you figure out who that is, follow through on the plan to make a brand-new you!

Before   After

OPTION 1: Be Mr. or Miss Outgoing.

1. Have 'em at hello.

Movie stars become famous by getting their faces out there. You can't turn into "someone" until people see you, so introduce yourself and show them who you are. The more people you meet, the more interesting a "character" you become.

2. A better form of global warming.

Break the ice. Don't know what to say? Ask people about their favorite subject—themselves! Then you don't have to talk—*they* do. Other possible topics: school stuff ("What is up with Mr. Odenkirk's hair?"); cultural stuff ("Can you *believe* what [crazy celebrity] did?")…you get the idea.

OPTION 2: Be an A student.

1. Keep your eyes on the prize.

How many A's do you want? Is there a subject you're itching to ace, or do you want to see a perfect column of straight A's on your report card? Write down your goal, and stick it where you'll be reminded of it regularly.

② Get in on the secrets.

Pssst…they're all around you! Watch what the A students in your class do and follow suit. Here are a few grade-A habits you might consider picking up:

- *Don't stop for anything at homework time. Put the magazine away. Don't IM till you've done your work. Your hair looks good, quit restyling it!*

- *Just do it. Do all your homework, all the time. Yeah, it may feel like busywork. Yeah, you may get some of it wrong. Big deal. Just put in your best effort and get 'er done.*

- *If you can't figure something out yourself, get help. Even top students get confused sometimes.*

3 Don't give up.

It can take more than one semester to make the transformation to star student, especially if you set your sights super high. Give it time, and keep taking steps—even little ones—up the grading alphabet.

How *Not* to Remake Your Rep

Watch out for these potholes on the road to the New You.

- **Going over the top.** You know those little dogs that don't stop barking? They make you want to yell, "Shut it, yappy!" Never try so hard that you're viewed as that pooch. Sometimes muzzling is a better strategy.

- **Pretending to be what you're not.** When friends change, you might want to remake your image, too. But if you're uncomfortable with the new and "improved" you, you can always switch back to the "classic" version.

- **Ditching someone because they seem like a bad fit with your new image.** One reputation you *don't* want is "person who leaves behind her friends."

How to Stop a Rumor in Its Tracks

OMG! LOL! Did you hear? This kid totally cut one in the middle of Spanish class yesterday! Isn't that hilarious? Uh, yeah. Except, it isn't true...and the kid everyone is talking about is *you*. Time to act fast, or spend the rest of the week (or more!) known as "El Gasso Supremo."

OPTION 1: Nip it in the bud.

1 Do some sleuthing.

Ask the person spreading the rumor who *he* heard it from, and then ask *that* person who *she* heard it from, and follow up with *that* person who *he* heard it from, until you find out who started the rumor mill turning. Then...

2 Take action.

No one wants to be known as the town gossip, so talk to Rumor Starter privately. Once *he* knows that *you* know he made up stories about your mom wearing earplugs while you play guitar, the jabbering will stop in a snap.

OPTION 2: Make the rumor mill work for you.

1 Start the chatterers chattering about the truth.

No, you did not beg, plead, or bribe your math teacher to give you a better grade on your test. And *no*, you did not curl up on the floor and start crying like a baby to get your way! But if you *did* have a question about your

Rumor vs. Reality

Rumor Version A   Rumor Version B   Reality

score and wanted to get it cleared up, don't let rumor-mongers turn it into something else.

Spread the truth: Let the gossip girls—and boys—know that you were standing up for yourself. And just as you won't let that not-so-great grade stand, you're not going to let an untrue rumor about you linger around the halls, either.

How to Survive E-mail Disasters

Can you imagine life without e-mail? Most of the time, it seems like one of the best things in the world—until the day you accidentally forward a message to the wrong person or reply in a rage. These tips will help keep you from making that one click you wish you could un-click.

1 Follow the "To" rules.

Write your e-mail first, *then* type in the person's address. That way, if you accidentally hit "send" partway through writing, it's only road kill on the information super-highway, and you're not the dead meat.

2 Delete the e-anger.

You know how in school, bad deeds go on your "per-manent record"? Well, the same goes for e-mailing mid freak-out: The receiver has a permanent record of your meltdown. When steam is pouring out of your ears, chill till it's all gone. *Then* write that e-mail.

③ LOL to the rescue.

Sometimes e-mail can be hard to read—and not just b/c u cn't undrstnd the msg. An "obvs joke" to you isn't always clear to someone else. An emoticon can be a quick way to show you're kidding: ;), :P, :>), or just say you're LOLing.

④ Step away from the computer.

If your e-blooper can't be emoticonned away, pick up that crazy talking box known as the telephone and call your friend. Explain what you really meant, and apologize if she got the wrong idea.

Defending Your Inbox

You wouldn't invite a vampire into your home, so don't let an evil creep get into your inbox.

- **Ban bullies.** Exile nasty e-mailers to deepest cyberspace by using the "Block Sender" option. Or get yourself a new e-mail addy and only give it to your trusted friends. (You've wanted to change up that old addy for a while, right?)

- **Keep it healthy.** Unfamiliar e-mail addresses with attachments are almost always bad news. Trash those messages ASAP, and then empty your garbage bin to stop a lurking virus in its tracks.

- **Shout it out.** Your virtual privacy is important, but if you get an e-mail that's extra weird, scary, or mean-spirited, show it to a parent or another adult.

How to Survive Having Your Sibling at School

When you were chasing the ice-cream truck last summer, your shorts split wide open. (Exactly the kind of story you don't want anyone at school to know!) Luckily, the only person who *does* know is your older...uh-oh.

Having a brother or sister sharing the school hallways can cause some serious complications. But with the right strategy, you can make your sib work for you!

1 ## Make an "I won't tell if you won't" pact.

Your sister also wants to keep *her* reputation intact, so propose a contract: She doesn't share the shorts story, and you'll keep her fear of chickens under wraps.

2 ## What happens at school stays at school.

Tattle on your brother, and you're just asking for him to tattle on you back. Don't tell Mom he used the teachers' lounge soda machine today. That way he won't mention the food fight you get in tomorrow.

3 ## Be relative-ly helpful.

Shocking but true—older brothers and sisters can be your secret weapon! Since they've *been there* and *done that*, they can provide inside info on tests, teachers, and what not to wear.

4 ## He's small, but significant.

A younger sibling can be useful, too. Make a big show of helping your little brother carry his diorama into school. Friends, teachers, and crushes will be impressed with what a great big sib you are…even if you secretly want to strangle him.

WORST NIGHTMARE

Your sister was such a rock star at school, people have pictures of *her* in their lockers. Your brother won the academic decathlon, was class president, and led the football team to the championship.

MY OLDER SIBLING WENT HERE, AND NO ONE WILL LET ME FORGET IT!

But people don't even bother to learn your name—they just call you "number two." No matter what you do, it feels like you just can't compare...

But guess what? You don't have to. You're your own person, so instead of living in your sib's shadow, make your own mark. Show people your personality and talents, and soon they'll just talk about *your* ability to shine.

And if one of your teachers keeps blah-blah-blahing about a certain someone in your house, have a private convo and let her know that you love your sib, but you prefer not to be compared.

How to Survive a Crush Without Getting Crushed

Love songs make it sound great, but thinking about your crush makes you a woozy, sweaty, nervous wreck. How wonderful! Want to get from liking someone to actually *talking* to that person? Read on.

① Play a game of Q&A.

When you see your crush, the only thing that usually comes out of your mouth is a string of drool. Instead of acting like a salivating puppy, ask your crush questions. They give you something to say besides, "Duh…uh…so…um…" and help you get to know the person better. Check these out:

- *What's your favorite flavor of gum?*
- *Can you blow a bubble inside a bubble?*
- *I just heard that the ability to roll your tongue is genetic—can you do it?*

Knowing what your cutie's into helps, too. Look for clues: Sneak a peek at your crush's binder or bag—any stickers for bands you haven't heard of? That's a question waiting to be asked!

② Cue the compliments.

"Your solo in chorus was so good!" or, "You can always make me laugh!" (Who doesn't want to hear that, right?) Avoid compliments about your crush's body, which might make you *both* embarrassed. Focus on stuff your crush *has done*, like scoring a goal or solving the "unsolvable" pre-algebra problem.

WORST NIGHTMARE

Not only did you hear that the person *you* like likes someone else…but the like-ee is your BFF.

THE PERSON I'M CRUSHING ON HAS A CRUSH ON MY BEST FRIEND!

- **Get real.** Telling your friend, "Eyes off my crush," won't work—if *you* can't stop looking at this person, how can you expect anyone else to?

- **Get fit.** While your friend and your crush are busy IMing, use the time to run some laps, hit the pool, or do another activity to take your mind off the problem. It will also make for a stronger new you.

- **Get a grip.** Some people might say stuff like, "You must be so mad at her!" Remember: You're not really mad at your *friend*, just at the situation, so stay chill.

❸ Join the posse.

Look for an open spot at your crush's lunch table and join in the group conversation. Then talk to *everybody*, not just your crush. Sometimes hanging with friends helps make everyone more comfortable.

❹ iChat, uChat.

Like they say in tennis, it's "advantage" you if you e-mail or IM your crush. That way, you start the dialogue when you're ready, and respond when you have the perfect answer. Plus, your crush can't see if you're nervous! To start the e-convo, use the questions-and-compliments strategy. "Hey, your art project was amazing," or, "What are we supposed to bring for social studies tomorrow?"

> **BE AWARE •** If your crush isn't responding, whether online or in person, don't freak: There are a million possible reasons for the silence. (Be patient!) Besides, someone else might have a crush on *you*—anyone asking you a lot of questions lately?

How to Stay Out of a Fight

Someone says something mean. You yell right back. The words start coming fast, hard, and hurtful. Before you know it, a full-scale fight is in full-swing. But wait! Back up. It doesn't have to be that way. Here's how to step away from a scuffle before fists fly.

❶ Take the temperature.

Before a fight explodes, you'll usually see sparks. Look for these warning signs:

- *Angry stares*
- *Sudden movements, like books slamming down or lockers shutting noisily*
- *A gathering crowd*
- *A kick, shove, pinch, or other dis that goes over the top*
- *Someone shouting, "Oh, it is so on!"*

❷ Walk away (with honor).

Stop the fight *before* it begins. Say, "I don't want to fight you." Be firm, then walk away. Now focus on relaxing and breathing slowly, feeling confident that you've won because you didn't give that hothead the "pleasure" of a fight.

❸ Know *yourself.*

Pay attention to the way you feel before you blow your fuse. Is your heart racing, or is your voice getting louder? When those things start to happen—even for tiny reasons, like someone else getting the last slice of pizza in the cafeteria line—find a way to release steam.

How to Blow Off Some Steam

When you feel *this* close to a shouting match (or worse), here's how to divert your anger.

- **Breathe.** Sounds easy, right? Try to inhale for five seconds, then exhale for five. These are called "cleansing breaths," because they can vacuum out some anger.

- **Keep a stress reliever in your locker,** like a foam ball you can squeeze, and have at that baby till your hand hurts.

- **During lunch,** exorcise with exercise!

Still in a huff when you get home?

- **Tunes to the rescue.** Play some of the *loudest*, most *obnoxious* songs you can, and scream along!

- **Write the day down.** List every detail, from what got you mad to who said what, when. Later, see if the "older" you agrees with how the you of today dealt with things.

CHAPTER 4

For Boys Only!

How to Survive Being the Shortest Guy in School

Everyone else has been doing some *serious* growing, but your body hasn't gotten the message. Suddenly every boy in school towers over you—and so do some of the girls. Here are some tips to keep you from feeling shortchanged.

1 Learn some good short jokes.

Make up for what you lack in altitude with the right attitude. Even if it drives you crazy on the inside, never show that being short is a problem for you.

- *"I'm short on purpose. If the teacher can't see you, he can't call on you!"*
- *"At least if I fall down, I don't have far to go."*
- *"I'm not short, I'm just unusually not tall."*
- *"You just wait till the limbo contest, my friend…you just wait."*

❷ Consider the advantages.

Take comfort in the good news from scientists: Short people live longer and break fewer bones. Plus, they're less clumsy and have faster reaction times. So play point guard during basketball games or try out for soccer goalie, and show 'em what "that short dude" can do.

FAST FACT • Short people are often better at weight lifting because they don't have to lift the weights as far!

Long on Accomplishment

Though short in stature, these guys stand tall in history:

- **Roger Daltrey.** Lead singer of The Who. Member of the Rock and Roll Hall of Fame. Five feet, seven inches tall.

- **Napoleon Bonaparte.** Ruled France. Conquered half of Europe. Five feet, six and a half inches tall.

- **Salvador Dalí.** Brilliant Spanish surrealist painter. Five feet, seven inches tall.

How to Survive Not Being Athletic

Gym class is the same every day: There are guys beating the school record in the 1,600-meter run, guys making perfect corner kicks, guys shooting hoops like they're ready for the pros. And then there's you: dropping every ball, doubled over to catch your breath. Before you throw in the towel, read on.

1. Practice makes perfect.

What makes most good athletes good isn't a natural gift, it's how much they practice. Find a buddy who's more confident than you on the field and drill him about how he got that way. Does he play soccer in his neighborhood after school? Run around the track with his dad in the mornings? Do twenty push-ups before bed every night?

2. Incorporate sports into your daily life.

Run up the stairs instead of walking, and keep a record of your time so you can attempt to beat it tomorrow. When you have a milk carton to throw in the garbage, do it from across the room with a beat-the-buzzer jump shot. When you're alone, make up goofy sports to practice, like Race the Dog or Hurdle the Patio Furniture.

3. Mix it up.

Playing sports doesn't have to mean hitting a ball, so try something different. Hit the local pool on the weekend and swim some laps, dig your old bike out of the garage and zip around the neighborhood, or try out some new tricks at the local skateboard park.

Finding *one* athletic activity that you're good at—or at least not terrible at—will boost your confidence with sports in general.

4 Take a reality check.

The truth is that *most* guys aren't super-amazing athletes, so not being Joe Sportsman only makes you (gasp!) normal.

Garden of Late Bloomers

Think you're never going to be any good? Think again—these sports superstars didn't start shining until they were practically old enough to retire.

- **"Big Bill" Tilden** ended up as one of the best tennis players of the 20th century, but he wasn't good enough to make his high-school squad.

- Hall of Fame pitcher **Dazzy Vance** didn't win his first baseball game until he was 31.

- **Sandy Koufax** almost quit baseball to go into the electronics business at the age of 25. But Koufax decided to give it one more shot. By the end of the 1961 season, he was on his way to being one of baseball's best pitchers.

- Super Bowl champion quarterback **Kurt Warner** didn't even enter the NFL until he was 28.

How to Survive a Bad Haircut

A great haircut is like getting a whole new you. Unfortunately, a bad haircut does the same thing, except now, the New You looks like you got into a fight with a lawn mower...and the mower won. Here are a few tips to restore your hair to sanity.

1 Bust out the products.

Rock stars of both genders use gel, so raid your mother's or sister's supplies: styling gel, mousse, wax, modeling

MULLET BOWL SPIKE MOHAWK

clay…whatever it takes. Then be sure to ask the product's owner how to apply it, because you don't want to go overboard with the "wet" look.

② Start a fad.

Tell all your pals that your hideous, horrible hairstyle is the hot new 'do. Let them know this is *exactly* how you wanted it to look because, yes, you are just that punk rawk!

③ If you can't beat it, buzz it!

Sometimes a hairdo's so bad it requires a 'do-over. So stop cursing yourself when you look in the mirror. Instead, take action! Go back to the salon and ask for a chopper fixer-upper—even if that means it all goes.

④ Let it go, let it grow.

Did you know your hair will grow half a foot this year?! So no matter how bad the current cut, the good news is that it's already growing out. You'll be looking better in no time—but until then, one further idea: Caps are cool. Start wearing a hat and it may soon be your *thing*!

How to Survive a Bully

He calls you names from the back of the bus. He trips you in the cafeteria. When he passes by with his posse of fools, they get all up in your grill. None of this is cool or acceptable, so here are ways to make it better…and to make it stop.

① Poker-face it.

It's like what dentists say about teeth: "Ignore them and they'll go away." Same here. By playing it cool and showing this bully that you're not bothered by his antics, he might just decide you're not worth his time and effort.

> **BE AWARE •** The most hardened bullies may be determined to break a poker face, so you may need to supplement this technique with a vanishing act (see #4).

WORST NIGHTMARE

You've been shoved—and smack into the girl you were trying to impress!

A BULLY SHOVED ME RIGHT INTO MY CRUSH!

- **Make her laugh.** "Did you know the halls are full of alligators that trip people to eat their fallen books?"

- **Check her out.** If your crush helps you collect your books, you know she's a good gal. If she teases you, forget about her.

❷ Launch a counterintelligence operation.

Secretly spy on the bully for a couple days, noting where he hangs out and when. The best way to steer clear is to know where he's going to be—and *not* be there yourself!

❸ Use the buddy system.

Get your friends together and coordinate your schedules so that none of you ever shows your face in the hallways alone. Bullies are much less likely to hassle two people together than one person alone.

❹ Make a quick escape.

Make a mental map of your school, and when the bully starts to bug you, move quickly to a "safe zone" (i.e., somewhere with adults around, if necessary). In case anybody calls you on running away, be ready with a smart remark: "I decided not to waste my time with that. Trust me, you shouldn't either." Or there's always: "Well, if you want in on the action, feel free to deal with the situation for me."

⑤ Be brave—or *fake* being brave.

Stand up to the bully. That's right: Tell him you want him to stop being mean to you. Say, "Bullying is very elementary school, and I'm over it." It often works best if you can do this when you and he can't be over-heard, so he doesn't feel like he has to prove himself. Be strong and act like you have authority. It's amazing how sometimes even just acting the part helps you assume the role.

⑥ Tell (without telling that you told).

No one wants to be a tattletale, but, um, no one wants to get punched in the face, either. Talk with a parent, teacher, counselor, or other trusted adult and ask for help solving this problem—*without* anyone knowing that you told.

Or send an anonymous e-mail or note to the vice principal or another authority figure at your school about how a certain kid is harassing a certain other kid every day at a certain place and time. And, what do you know? The next time the bully is doing his nasty thing, here comes trouble—for *him*.

How to Deal with Girl Confusion

Sure, science is rough, but the most confusing subject at school is easily *girls*. Not just girls—*the* Girl. She travels with her friends in a whispering and giggling pack, looking at you every once in a while, sometimes ignoring you, sometimes saying "hi" like it's no big deal.... How can you decode her mysterious, mind-boggling ways? Here's how to figure her out.

PART 1: Does she like you?

You know you like her, if you define "like" as being mesmerized by the way her hair bounces. But is it a two-way street? Look for these good signs.

She can't stop twirling her hair.

She's always fidgeting, flipping her hair, or scratching her nose while you're having a conversation. Chances are her twitchiness is not an allergic reaction. It's very possible she's looking for something to do with her hands because she's been attacked by a case of nerves. Why? 'Cause she digs you and wants to make a good impression!

She talks to you for random reasons.

She makes fun of your outfit, no matter what you're wearing. She wants help with the math assignment, even though she's an A student and you can't tell a prime number from a prime rib. She wants to use your pencil sharpener, but she's using a pen.

She laughs at your lamest jokes.

If you say that six is afraid of seven because seven ate nine, and she cracks up—she either likes you or she's got the worst sense of humor in the universe.

PART 2: How to hang out with her.

Avoid "playful" insults and jokes.

Instead, find out what interests her. Do you have any knowledge about her interests that you could share? If not, why not try to read up a bit? It's a pretty cool way to gain friendship *and* IQ points.

Compliments are key.

By telling her how cool her locker decorations are or that you agreed with what she said in class, you let her know that she's making an impression, and it's a good one!

Take it online.

IMs and e-mail are perfect for getting to know some-one without the stress of actual, in-person communi-cation. So ask for her e-mail address and screenname, and chat away! Next time you see her in person, bring up the topic of your last online convo, so you have a bridge from the e-world to the *real* world.

Eight Things to Talk About with Your Crush When You Don't Know What to Say

- How bad (or good) the food is at school.

- How hard (or easy) Mr. Wolfson's class is.

- How lame (or cool) the school dance was.

- What celebrity she hatey-hate-hates.

- What a pain your brother is—and ask her if *she* has any siblings.

- Bands you like—and ask what she likes, too.

- Best joke she's heard…and, yeah, be sure to LOL.

- Movies you saw recently—and…oh, you get the picture.

CHAPTER 5

For Girls Only!

How to Survive Mean Girls

There's no saying what turns a girl mean, though scientists have their theories.

- *Theory #1 suggests that deep down, the girl is insecure and knows she's not as cool as she's pretending to be.*
- *Theory #2 proposes that a mean girl is like social spinach: She's been put here to make you stronger.*
- *Theory #3 states that she's mean because her jeans are too tight and they're cutting off the oxygen to her brain.*

Whatever the cause, a mean girl's nasty ways don't have to get you down. Here's how to deal with the most common species.

THE TWO-FACED FRIEND

She tells you that she loves your outfit, wants to make plans with you after school, and agrees with everything you say…then she turns around and says the exact opposite to the girl she suddenly decides she likes more than you.

Don't get hysterical.

Going bananas will only give this girl gossip fuel to report back to others. Talk to her with a cool head and calm heart instead.

 ### Talk trust.

Tell The Mirror Has Two Faces that you know what's going on. Then ask her to play it straight with you because you *want* to trust her.

 ### Suggest "rep protection."

Explain that people often think badly of folks who say one thing and then do another. Tell her you don't want to see her become the girl whose word means squat.

THE CRITICIZER

"What are you wearing?!" she asks. Or she criticizes your favorite song and says you won't "get it" when you ask what hers is.

 ## Banish her bad-mouthing.

Now let her know that you'd appreciate it if she'd keep her negative thoughts to herself. Even better: laugh it off.

 ## Blah, blah, blah... *whatever!*

First, get her voice out of your head! Feel confident about your strengths and tastes, and you'll find her cutting comments actually mean less than a speck of glitter.

THE SECRET SPILLER

This friend crosses her heart, hopes to die, says she'll stick a needle in her eye if she betrays you. Then, two minutes later, the banshee screams your secrets to anyone who will listen!

 ### Zip her lip.

Remind Lady Overshare that you're counting on her to stay silent, and if she blabs, you can't trust her again.

 ### Protect yourself.

If you've been burned more than once, you might have to accept that the girl's got diarrhea of the mouth. Look for another person to tell the things you really want to stay between you and your confidante.

QUEEN MEAN

Though she's nice to you, your good friend can be a witch on wheels to others. Since friends don't let friends stay wicked, let her know it's time to lose the 'tude.

 Girl down!

Tell Miss Mean Jeans that when she's rude, it makes *you* feel bad. Let her know her words can come out harsher than she thinks, and you don't want someone to get hurt unintentionally.

 Model behavior.

Through your good example, show her that cruelty's not cool. Behaving with kindness might not only help make her nicer, but it might also win *you* new friends.

How to Survive a Best-Friend Breakup

You hung out all summer. You even helped her choose the great outfit she wore on the first day of school. And now she's suddenly hanging out with new people, and you've been dumped like a dirty diaper. Whaddaya do?

① I will survive!

First, understand that you're not alone. This is one of those lame life things that everyone eventually endures. But endure it you will, and things *will* turn around.

2 Stick your neck out.

You may want to pull a turtle, but don't retreat from the world! The sooner you open yourself up to new friend-ships with new girls—ones who might even share more of your interests than your old BFF—the sooner you'll feel better.

3 Be a joiner.

Now's the perfect time to try out for the soccer team. Or join yearbook. Or *parlez français* in French club. Think about it: You'll already have something in com-mon with the people in the group, so chances are you'll meet some fun, new friends while doing some-thing you enjoy.

4 Be bold.

Take a leap and ask someone new to the movies or another fun event. It may seem uncomfortable at first, but it's really no big deal. You can even follow this script word for word: "Hi, [name]! I'm going to see [movie name] this weekend, and was wondering if you wanted to come?"

5 Be patient…she may come back!

If you haven't already figured this out, middle school can be a time that's "krazy" with a "k." People change on a daily basis, both physically and mentally. Just because you aren't feeling love from the BFF right now doesn't mean all is lost. This could just be an ugly phase, so stay chill, keep living your life, and have fun. If your friend doesn't realize what she's missing, she might not be as smart as you thought she was.

Horribly Heinous BFF Breakups

- L8R LUZR! Your BFF dumps you via text message, and lets you know she never wants to talk to you again...with angry *emoticons*.

- You get uninvited to her birthday party...and she's your identical twin!

- Her new BFF pronounces your name wrong, and your old BFF adopts the pronunciation.

- She IMs your mom, but not you.

- She "breaks up" with you, and then starts hanging out with your older brother.

How to Deal with a Boy Bothering You

Sometimes it's hard to tell if the attention you get from a boy is because he really, really likes you or because he really, really *dislikes* you. (Boys remain very much like their cavemen ancestors in this way: "Me hungry! Me tired! Me bad at social interaction!")

Since you can't climb into a boy's head to learn what he's really thinking, let him know his bad behavior has got to stop.

Field Guide to Bothersome Boys

BEHAVIORS:

Takes food off your tray in the cafeteria and eats it.

Puts a "KICK ME" sign on your back.

Throws things in your hair.

Tries to yank your shorts down in gym.

1 Use "uh-uh, that ain't cool" body language.

If you don't want to talk to him, a gesture can be worth a thousand words.

2 Tell him straight.

How's this for easy: Just say, "Hey, [boy's name], please stop." It's short. It's sweet. And it should let him know that you're sick of his immature behavior. What happens if he keeps up with the baloney after you've told him to stop? Your next response is not to respond at all. That's right: Freeze him out. Let him know he can take it down the road because you're not buying anything he's selling. Boys *looooove* attention, and if you stop giving it to them, chances are they'll just go seek out another target who will.

3 Try the once-and-for-all.

Now, for a girl who wants to give Boy a little taste of his own medicine, she can try this line: "You sure are spending a lot of time and energy on li'l old me. Everyone knows it's because you have a crush on me." If you serve *that* one up, it'll not only stop the boy in his tracks, it might even make him quake in his sneakers.

Field Guide to Body Language

The dismissively deadly "Whatever" hair flip

The "Oh, you can't be serious" head shake

The eye roll that screams, "It's a shame you're so immature!"

The "I'm not impressed" lip flutter

The turned-up palms that ask, "Are you kidding me? Seriously, are you kidding me?"

How to Cope When a Clique Shuts You Out

Middle school can be as cruel as that old saying about fashion: "One day you're in, the next day you're out." If you're no longer welcome at your old lunch table, or if you don't get the call for the shopping expedition, it can make you feel like you've been "*auf*ed." (As in: "So long, farewell, *auf Wiedersehen*, good-bye.") Suddenly you're an outcast, forced to wander the mine field that is the school cafeteria. What do you do?

1 Dopes mope.

Unfortunately, this sitch is not going to improve until *you* make it happen. Don't sit around waiting for reacceptance. Even if you have to *force* yourself to smile, try it. Research shows that smiling actually makes you feel better. Truly. Give it a shot…no, don't stop yet. You have to keep doing it. Uh-huh. Yes, that's it. There you go…

② Become a "Say cheese!" whiz.

Get involved in an activity that draws people to you. Everybody loves to have their picture taken, so join the school yearbook staff and start clicking. Or start a band if you play an instrument. If you like to cook, share samples of your best work at lunch. Local museums often offer courses, so take an art class in a fab new setting. These activities should not only be fun, but they'll also boost your confidence and send some well-earned attention your way. And, yeah: Your old crowd will definitely realize what it's missing!

3 One-on-one.

Though it's nice to be part of a group, the best friendship moments often come when you're doing something fun with just one good friend. Now's the perfect time to "remeet" one of the *chicas* in your class that you've known forever but haven't hung out with in a while (or ever!). Make a plan to do something fun together. Or imagine how thrilled the new girl who just moved to town would be if you invited her to the movies. Middle school is your time to explore all sorts of new things, and pairing up with a new friend is a great way to start.

WORST NIGHTMARE

It's Saturday night and all of your friends are getting ready to go to *the* party of the year...to which you weren't invited. How will you cope? You can have an equally great night! (Haven't you ever heard of a "party of one"?)

EVERYONE WAS INVITED TO THE PARTY...EXCEPT ME!

First, fix yourself a healthy beverage (smoothie, anyone?), then head to the bathroom. Turn on some tunes, drop some bubble bath in the tub, and once the water gets thick with suds, climb in and relax. Soak until you've turned into a human prune, or until another family member starts banging on the door and demands you get out. Once you've dried off, file your nails, buff your feet, and apply polish to all twenty digits. By the end of the night, you'll be completely chillaxed and gorgeous!

How to Handle Wardrobe Emergencies

Oh. My. Gosh! You walked out of your house, got on the bus, and made it halfway down the hall to homeroom before you were clued in to the fact that your shirt is practically see-through, and *everyone* can see the bumblebee pattern on your bra! Or you sat on some paint in art class, and the whole school thinks you got your you-know-what.

Ugh! Ugh! Ugh! And it demands to be said again: *Uuuggghhh!*

Wardrobe disasters can make you want to crawl under your desk and stay there till the final bell rings. But if you remember these tricks, you'll be able to hold your head up without wanting to barf all over your shirt (which would be another monstrous mishap).

① Pinky promise.

Make a pact with one friend—your "go-to girl" who can be trusted *completely*—that you will tell each other if a funky stain ever materializes on your butt, or if your shirt is transparent. If your girl whispers, "Damage!" proceed to #2.

② Locker up.

No, this doesn't mean hide in your locker. It means that you were given a locker for just such emergencies, so keep an extra sweater or hoodie in there (or at the bottom of your book bag). Once you have that extra piece of clothing safely in hand, wrap it around your waist or over your shirt, and *voilà*! Problem solved!

Locker Up

ready-for-anything box with mints, hair ties, lip balm, and lotion

magnetic mirror to see how cute you look

extra sweater or hoodie for covering up in case of disaster

photos of you and your friends having fun OUTSIDE of school

extra pair of shoes for new-shoe blister agony

top-secret box with personal hygiene stuff

3 Store secret supplies.

Someone you know (possibly even you) will get her period at school. Rather than being caught unprepared, do yourself a favor and keep some supplies in a non-see-through pencil case in your purse, book bag, or in the back of your locker. That way, if Aunt Flow visits you or your friend during the school day, you can minimize the mortification.

4 Presto, change-o!

A classic magician's trick can also be of use to you: Distract attention! You never see a magician switching a coin from one hand to another because he has drawn your eyes elsewhere. Keep a candy necklace or big plastic ring in a supply box in your locker, and pop it on so that if people start staring, they'll focus on the delicious candy around your neck, not the stain on your jeans.

5 Professional help.

If all else fails, the school nurse or a female teacher often has stuff that can help in a pinch. Since these pros have seen it all before, you can feel comfortable asking them for assistance if you need it.

How to Survive When a Secret Gets Out

Secrets can be tough to keep secret, especially if you share them in a public place where you can be (wince) overheard! If you find you've said too much at just the wrong time, here's how to deal.

1 Don't be "crushed."

Your crush rolls up just as you're confessing how much you like him. *Whoops!* After the color of your face downgrades from purple to pink, smile at him. Say something like, "Okay, so yes: I said you're cute, because you are. That's your compliment for the day. You may now feel free to compliment me anytime you'd like." And with that, walk away. *Ha-cha!*

2 Request respect.

You can't take your words back, but you *can* gently remind whoever overheard that the info is *private*. Tell them that you trust they're good at keeping secrets.

Zip it up in the bathroom.

To avoid future secret spills, beware of talking privately in places where unseen listeners can lurk. Don't assume you're alone in the girls' room just because you don't see anyone. Same goes for stairwells—you never know who's on the next landing.

Appendix

SOME STEPS TO HELP YOU THROUGH A SCHOOL DANCE

The Running Man

1. Put your left foot forward while sliding your right foot backward.
2. Put your right foot forward while sliding your left foot backward.
3. Repeat.
4. Look: You're running!
5. Change direction! Wave at passersby!
6. Oh no! A mean dog is chasing you! Run faster!

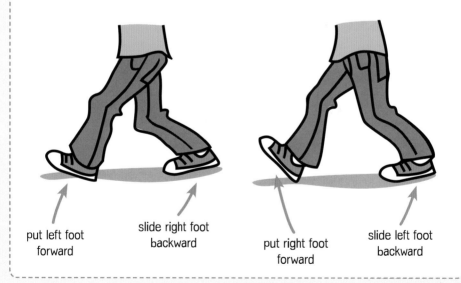

put left foot forward   slide right foot backward   put right foot forward   slide left foot backward

The Lawn Mower

1. Bend down and grab the starter cord.

2. Pull the starter cord up and to the left! Again! Again!

3. Grab the imaginary handle of the mower.

4. Bring your left foot forward. Right foot forward.

5. Look: You're pushing a lawn mower!

6. Wipe a bead of sweat from your brow. Dodge a bee! Drink some water!

7. And you're mowing again!

wipe "sweat" from your brow

grab the starter cord and pull back

grab an imaginary handle

bring your left foot forward

bring your right foot forward

The Funky Chicken

1. Stand with your feet slightly apart.
2. Tuck your hands into your armpits—now your arms are wings!
3. Raise your right "wing" as you kick out your left leg.
4. Bring your right wing down as you bring your left leg back in.
5. Repeat with your other wing and leg.
6. Rapidly bob your head up and down, like a chicken pecking at grain.
7. Oh no! It's the farmer! He's got an ax! Flap as hard as you can to get away!

rapidly bob head up and down

raise right "wing"

kick out left leg

Appendix

HOW TO DEAL WITH PIMPLES

Here's what to do when the pimple fairy dumps a big, fat, disgusting one on your face.

Zit Hiding

Holding an ice cube against a pimple reduces the inflammation. Once that volcano is smaller, ask a makeup pro (like your mom or sister) to help you conceal it. Look for a concealer that matches your skin tone (it might take a few tries before you get it right).

Zit Prevention

The more you touch your face, the more dirt and oil you rub in—so hands off! Fight the urge to pick, prick, or pop. And *no* squeezing that blemish, because it'll only get worse.

Finally, wash your face twice (and *only twice*) a day with warm water and gentle soap or cleanser. Wash any more and you'll risk irritating your skin.

BE AWARE • If things get really bad, ask to see a dermatologist who'll banish the bumps professionally.

Appendix

HOW TO PACK YOUR BACKPACK WITHOUT CRACKING YOUR BACK

1. Put your heaviest, biggest book in first, standing upright in the back of your bag, so you feel one big flat surface against your back, instead of a bunch of lumpy little things and book corners poking you.
2. Stack your other big, fat textbooks horizontally on the bottom of the bag.
3. Pack lighter stuff next: gym clothes, workbooks, paperback textbooks, and notebooks.
4. On the very top goes your lunch or snack, and anything else that's ruined if smushed, like that clay project you're taking home from art class.

- **Secure pockets** are for anything that you're going to be toast if you lose: calculator, cell phone, keys, that little piece of paper you've got your locker combo on.

- **Easy-access pockets** are where you put things you're going to need fast, like a pencil case or water bottle.

The Neat Horizontal Stack-Up

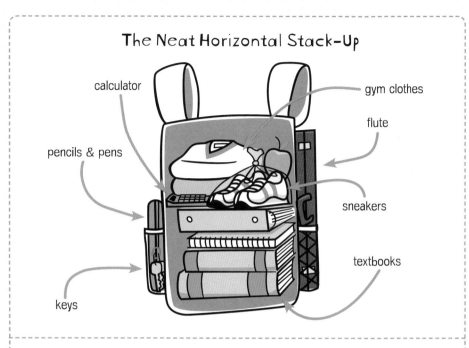

calculator

gym clothes

flute

pencils & pens

sneakers

keys

textbooks

The Total Mess

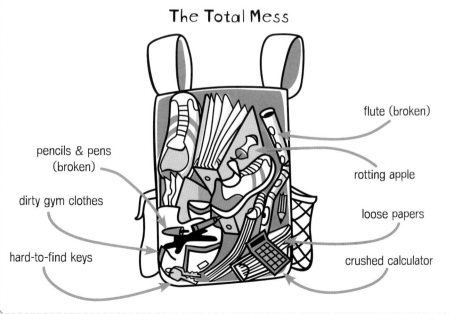

flute (broken)

pencils & pens (broken)

rotting apple

dirty gym clothes

loose papers

hard-to-find keys

crushed calculator

About the Authors

David Borgenicht is a writer, editor, publisher, and the coauthor of all the books in the Worst-Case Scenario Survival Handbook series. He lives in Philadelphia. David is happy to have survived middle school P.E., despite being designated the primary target in every dodgeball game.

Ben H. Winters lives in Brooklyn and writes books, plays, musicals, articles, and lots of to-do lists. In middle school, he was "angry man number three" in the school play of *Twelve Angry Men*.

Robin Epstein lives in Brooklyn and teaches writing at New York University. Thanks to her experience in 7th grade cooking class, she became determined never to cook again.

About the Illustrator
Chuck Gonzales is a New York City–based illustrator. In middle school, his dream of being a leading man was dashed when he had to play a dancing bag of garbage instead.